Introduction

Welcome to a Journey of Discovery

Dear reader,

Embarking on a journey to discover Japanese philosophy is like opening a door to a world where every detail, every gesture, and every thought has a profound meaning. Japanese culture, rich in ancient traditions and practical wisdom, offers valuable teachings for anyone seeking balance, inner peace, and a deeper understanding of themselves and the world.

Imagine walking through a Zen garden, where every stone has been carefully placed, every plant has been carefully chosen. This garden is an external reflection of an internal order, a visual representation of the harmony we can cultivate within ourselves. In this book, I will guide you through the cornerstones of Japanese philosophy, helping you discover how these ancient principles can be applied to your modern life to create lasting balance.

The Importance of Balance

The concept of balance, or "Wa," is at the heart of Japanese philosophy. In Japanese culture, balance is not just a goal, but a natural state from which everything must flow. This concept extends to every aspect of life: from interpersonal relationships to our connection with nature to the management of our thoughts and emotions.

In a world often characterized by excess and imbalance, the principle of Wa reminds us of the importance of living in harmony with everything around us. It is not just about finding a balance between work and personal life, but about creating an inner harmony that is reflected in our daily actions.

What to Expect

In this book, we will explore the foundations of Japanese philosophy together, starting with its roots in Zen Buddhism, Shinto, and Confucianism, and then exploring how these principles can guide your daily life. It won't be just theory; I'll provide practical exercises and inspiring stories to help you apply what you learn.

We will see how the Way of the Warrior, Bushidō, can teach us discipline and righteousness. We will explore the art of simplicity and beauty in imperfection with Wabi-Sabi, and discover our purpose in life through the concept of Ikigai. Each chapter will offer you personal reflections and practical tools to integrate these ancient teachings into your modern life.

At the end of this journey, I hope you can see the world with new, more aware eyes, and find within yourself the resources to live a more balanced and meaningful life.

Chapter 1: The Heart of Japanese Philosophy

Japanese philosophy is the result of a long process of assimilation and adaptation of cultural and religious influences from other parts of Asia. Although Japanese culture has developed its own unique identity, it cannot be fully understood without acknowledging the influences that Zen Buddhism, Shinto, and Confucianism have had on Japanese thought.

Zen Buddhism It arrived in Japan from China around the 6th century, and with it came a worldview that emphasized meditation, awareness of the present moment, and acceptance of impermanence. This thinking has permeated not only religion, but also Japanese art, culture, and daily life. The practice of Zazen meditation, for example, has become a central part of the lives of Zen monks and has influenced many other practices, such as the tea ceremony and the art of gardening.

Shintoism, Japan's native religion, is equally fundamental. With its emphasis on the sacredness of nature and the divine presence in every element of the natural world, Shinto has instilled a deep respect for nature at the heart of Japanese culture. Shinto rituals, which celebrate natural events such as the changing seasons, reflect a deep connection with the natural world, a connection that manifests itself in the daily lives of the Japanese.

Confucianism, which also came from China, provided an ethical and moral framework that profoundly influenced Japanese society. Its emphasis on respect for elders, loyalty, and correctness in social relationships has shaped family and community life in Japan, creating a culture that values social harmony and individual duty.

These three traditions have interacted with each other over the centuries, creating a philosophy that is both practical and deeply spiritual, capable of guiding every aspect of life, from daily interactions with others to the search for meaning in life.

Wa - The Harmony

The concept of **How** is central to Japanese life and represents the harmony that must exist between individuals, society, and nature. Wa is not just an abstract ideal; it is a practical guide for daily life. In interpersonal relationships, for example, maintaining Wa means avoiding conflict, promoting cooperation, and always acting with mutual respect. In society, Wa manifests itself in attention to the community, in the importance given to the common good, and in the search for a balance between various interests.

Nature is also seen as an element that must be lived in harmony with. In Japan, the construction of a garden or a house is never separated from consideration for the surrounding environment. Each element is designed to integrate with nature, not to dominate it. This respect for natural balance is also reflected in practices such as **Shinrin Yoku**, or "forest bathing," which emphasizes the importance of immersing oneself in nature to find inner peace.

Wabi-Sabi - The Beauty of Imperfection

In a world that often celebrates perfection and the new, the concept of **Wabi Sabi** offers us a radically different perspective. Wabi-Sabi is acceptance of imperfection, impermanence, and incompleteness as an essential part of beauty. This principle teaches us to find beauty in the cracks of a ceramic cup, the wrinkles of an old face, and the leaves that fall in autumn.

Wabi-Sabi is also an invitation to live with humility and simplicity. It is a reminder that material things, even when beautiful, are destined to deteriorate and pass away. However, this very impermanence can be a source of beauty and meaning. For example, the Japanese tea ceremony, which often uses ancient and worn utensils, celebrates this imperfect beauty, where every sign of wear tells a story and adds value to the object.

Applying Wabi-Sabi in daily life means learning to see imperfections not as flaws, but as signs of authenticity and character. It also means cultivating patience and self-acceptance, recognizing that the pursuit of perfection is an unattainable goal and that true beauty lies in the process of becoming itself.

Conclusion of the Chapter

This first chapter introduced us to the beating heart of Japanese philosophy, a world where harmony, impermanence, and imperfection are celebrated as fundamental pillars of life. As we progress through the next chapters, we will explore how these principles can be applied practically to improve ourselves, find our purpose, and live in harmony with everything around us.

Just like in a Zen garden, where every stone and every plant has its place, we too can find our place in the world, creating a life that reflects beauty and inner harmony.

Chapter 2: The Way of the Warrior (Bushidō)

The Samurai Code

The Way of the Warrior, known as**Bushido**, is a code of conduct that has guided Japanese samurai for centuries. Originating during the feudal period, Bushidō was not just a set of rules for combat, but a true way of life, which shaped the behavior, decisions and ethics of samurai in every aspect of their existence. This code has deep roots in Zen philosophy, Shintoism and Confucianism, integrating values such as honor, courage, justice and loyalty.

For the samurai, Bushidō represented the supreme ideal of how a man should conduct himself. It was not just about knowing how to fight with skill and discipline, but about living with deep moral rectitude, facing life and death with dignity. Although the times of the samurai are gone, the principles of Bushidō remain relevant.

even today, offering valuable lessons on how we can live with integrity and inner strength.

In modern life, Bushido can be interpreted as a guide to developing character and personal discipline. It can help us navigate everyday challenges with greater resilience and moral clarity, teaching us the importance of living by sound principles and always acting with honor. Let's delve into some of the key values of Bushido and see how they can be applied in our daily lives.

Justice (Gi) and Courage (Yu)

Justice (Gi) is one of the fundamental principles of Bushidō and refers to righteousness and fairness in actions. For the samurai, acting justly meant making decisions based on what is right and proper, without being influenced by personal interests or fears. Justice requires a clear mind and a resolute heart, capable of distinguishing between good and evil, and acting accordingly, even when this may involve personal sacrifice.

In modern life, the Gi principle can guide us to make ethical choices in all areas, whether it's personal relationships, business, or social issues. Acting justly means making decisions that reflect our core values, even when they're difficult or unpopular. For example, in business, it can mean resisting the temptation to take advantage of a situation at the expense of others, choosing instead to act fairly and transparently.

Courage (Yu) It is closely linked to justice, because to act rightly it is often necessary to be courageous. Courage, for the samurai, was not simply the lack of fear, but the ability to act despite fear, when they knew that what they were doing was right. This value manifests itself in the determination to face difficulties and dangers with serenity and determination, without running away from responsibilities.

Today, courage can be seen in the ability to stand up for what we believe in, even when we face criticism, risks, or personal challenges. It is courage that allows us to take new paths, face our fears, and continue pursuing our goals, even when the path is uncertain or difficult. It is also courage that pushes us to ask for help when we need it, recognizing our limitations and working to overcome them.

A modern example of how to apply Gi and Yu might be in a work situation where one must report bad behavior. It might be easier to remain silent and ignore the problem, but justice requires that one do what is right, even if it is difficult. Courage, in this case, is the strength to act and speak out, even knowing that there may be personal consequences.

Honor (Meiyo) and Respect (Rei)

Honor (Meiyo)was perhaps the most precious value for a samurai. Living with honor meant living in such a way that every action, word and thought reflected the utmost respect for oneself and for others. Honor was the measure of a samurai's virtue, his greatest treasure, so much so that losing honor could mean having to resort to seppuku, ritual suicide, to restore one's reputation and dignity.

In the modern context, honor is no longer tied to rigid codes of conduct, but remains a central value in building a respectable and dignified life. Living honorably today means being true to one's principles, acting with integrity, and keeping one's word. It also means being aware of how our actions affect others and doing our best to behave in a way that inspires respect and admiration.

Respect (King), another fundamental principle of Bushidō, is closely linked to honor. For the samurai, respect was a formal behavior that reflected their dignity and that of others. Respect was manifested in every interaction, from the way one addressed a superior person, to how one treated opponents on the field of battle.

battle. It was a way of life that demonstrated courtesy, humility, and consideration for others.

In our daily lives, respect is essential to building and maintaining healthy relationships. It involves recognizing the intrinsic value of each person and treating them accordingly. Respect can manifest itself in small gestures, such as listening attentively when someone speaks, or in more significant actions, such as acknowledging and appreciating the contributions of others, even when they differ from our own.

Honor and respect are the foundations of a balanced life and healthy relationships. When we act with honor, we build trust in ourselves and others, and when we treat others with respect, we build bridges of understanding and cooperation. Applying these principles in modern life means being aware of our actions and their implications, always seeking to behave in a way that reflects the best of ourselves.

An example of living according to Meiyo and Rei could be in the way we handle conflict. Instead of reacting with anger or defensiveness, we can choose to approach disagreements calmly and respectfully, seeking solutions that honor all parties involved. This approach not only resolves conflicts more effectively, but also strengthens relationships and mutual respect.

Conclusion of the Chapter

Bushido, the way of the warrior, offers much more than lessons in fighting; it is a code of conduct that can guide us toward a life of righteousness, courage, honor, and respect. In a world that often seems to lack strong moral principles, these values   can be beacons of light, helping us navigate life's challenges with dignity and inner strength.

Applying the principles of Gi, Yu, Meiyo, and Rei in our daily lives can help us become better people, build stronger relationships, and live with a sense of purpose and fulfillment. As we continue our journey through Japanese philosophy, we will see how these values intertwine with other principles and how together they can create a harmonious and meaningful life.

In the next chapter, we will explore Zen Buddhism and the art of living mindfully, discovering how mindfulness and meditation can contribute to our inner serenity and daily balance.

Chapter 3: Zen and the Art of Living

Introduction to Zen Buddhism

Zen Buddhism is one of the most influential schools of Buddhism in Japan, and its philosophy has deeply permeated Japanese culture, art, and daily life. Originating in India, Buddhism spread to China, where it met Taoism and gave birth to the Chan school, which was then brought to Japan in the 6th century and took the name of Zen.

Zen, unlike other forms of Buddhism, places particular emphasis on direct meditation and personal experience of reality, rather than scriptural study or elaborate rituals. The word Zen comes from the Sanskrit "dhyāna," meaning meditation, and refers to the central practice of this philosophy: the attainment of awareness and enlightenment through meditation.

Zen Buddhism flourished during the Kamakura period (1185-1333), a time of war and turmoil in Japan, when samurai adopted its principles to strengthen their mental and spiritual discipline. Zen has influenced many aspects of Japanese culture, from gardening to tea rituals, from painting to ceramics, always with a focus on simplicity, immediacy, and mindfulness.

Today, Zen is appreciated throughout the world not only as a spiritual practice, but also as a philosophy that offers practical tools for dealing with the challenges of modern life. Its practices teach us to live in the present, to let go of distractions, and to find serenity in the present moment, regardless of external circumstances.

Japanese Mindfulness (Zanshin)

One of the fundamental teachings of Zen is awareness of the present moment, often referred to as**Zanshin**in Japanese culture. Zanshin literally translates as "remaining mind" or "persistent mind" and refers to a state of full awareness and concentration on what one is doing, maintaining careful and constant vigilance.

Zanshin is particularly evident in Japanese martial arts, where it is essential to remain fully focused on the action, even after a blow has been struck, in order to be ready for whatever happens. However, this concept goes beyond combat and is applicable to every aspect of daily life.

Practicing Zanshin means being fully present in every moment, whether working, cooking, talking to someone, or simply walking. It is the art of living with total mental presence, without letting the mind wander into the past or future. This state of calm alertness allows us to act with greater precision, calm, and control, reducing stress and improving the quality of our lives.

Practical Examples of Zanshin in Daily Life:

- **During meals:**Instead of eating hastily or absentmindedly in front of the TV, practicing Zanshin means dedicating your attention to the food, appreciating the flavors, the textures, and the act of nourishing yourself. This not only improves digestion, but transforms the meal into a moment of awareness and gratitude.
- **In communication:**When you talk to someone, practicing Zanshin means truly listening, without thinking about what to say next or what you are going to do. This level of attentiveness improves the quality of relationships, creating a sense of respect and deeper connection.
- **In daily activities:**Whether you're washing dishes, gardening, or working on a project, bring your mind fully into the action. Take one step at a time, focusing only on what you're doing in that moment. This reduces feelings of being overwhelmed and increases the satisfaction that comes from completing tasks.

Practicing Zanshin requires discipline, but over time, it can transform the quality of your life. It's a way to find inner calm, reduce stress, and live with greater intentionality.

Zazen Meditation

The beating heart of Zen practice is Zazen meditation, which simply means "sitting meditation." Zazen is more than just a meditation technique; it is a direct experience of reality, a means of awakening to our true nature and seeing things as they are, without the distortions of the mind.

How to Practice Zazen:

1. **Finding a Quiet Place:**Choose a quiet place where you can sit comfortably without distractions. It can be on a meditation cushion (zafu) or a chair, as long as you can keep your back straight.
2. **Body Position:**Assume a stable position. If you are sitting on a cushion, cross your legs in the lotus or half lotus position. If you are in a chair, rest your feet on the floor. The hands are positioned in the shape of a "cosmic mudra," with the right hand on top of the left and the thumbs lightly touching, forming an oval.
3. **Breathing:**Focus on your breathing. Breathe naturally through your nose, allowing your attention to rest on the movement of your abdomen as it expands and contracts. Don't try to control your breathing, just observe it.
4. **Observation of the Mind:**During Zazen, it is normal for the mind to wander. When you notice that you are distracted, simply acknowledge the thought and gently bring it back to the breath. There is no need to judge yourself or try to block the thoughts. The goal is to observe the thoughts without clinging to them.
5. **Duration:**Start with 10-15 minute sessions, gradually increasing the duration as you become more comfortable. More experienced practitioners can meditate for 30-40 minutes or more.

Benefits of Zazen:

- **Mental Calm:**Zazen helps calm the mind, reducing anxiety and stress. Regular practice allows you to develop greater inner serenity, even in the most frenetic daily life situations.
- **Clarity and Concentration:**Meditation improves your ability to concentrate and mental clarity, helping you make decisions with greater awareness and precision.
- **Self Awareness:**Through Zazen, one develops a greater awareness of one's body, thoughts and emotions, allowing one to better understand oneself and one's reactions.
- **Acceptance:**Zazen teaches the art of acceptance, not only of what happens outside, but also of the thoughts and emotions that arise. This acceptance leads to a more balanced and less reactive life.

Incorporating Zazen into Daily Life:

The beauty of Zazen is that it doesn't require a lot of time or special equipment. You can practice Zazen anywhere, even for just a few minutes a day, and easily integrate it into your routine. For example, you might start your day with 10 minutes of Zazen to establish a foundation of calm and concentration, or end your day with a short session to relax and reflect.

Furthermore, the practice of Zazen can be carried into all daily activities, cultivating a mindfulness and presence in every moment. It is not just sitting meditation; it is a way of life, an art of being present in every aspect of life.

Conclusion of the Chapter

Zen Buddhism offers us powerful tools to live with greater awareness and serenity. Through the practice of Zanshin and Zazen meditation, we can cultivate a calm and alert mind, capable of facing life's challenges with balance and clarity. These practices not only improve our mental well-being, but they help us live in harmony with ourselves and the world around us.

In the next chapter, we will explore the concept of Ikigai, the reason for being, and how we can discover and live our purpose in life. Continue this journey with openness and curiosity, bringing with you the awareness and calm that Zen teaches us.

Chapter 4: Ikigai - The Reason for Being

Discovering Your Ikigai

THE'**Ikigai**is a concept deeply rooted in Japanese culture and represents the "reason for being," the reason why one gets up each morning. In an often hectic and distracting world, finding and cultivating one's Ikigai can be the key to a life full of meaning, balance and happiness.

The term Ikigai is composed of two Japanese words: "Iki," which means "life," and "gai," which translates to "value" or "purpose." So, Ikigai can be thought of as the value we place on our lives, that deep, personal reason that drives us to live with joy and purpose. It's not simply about following a passion or pursuing a career; Ikigai is a unique combination of what you love, what you're good at, what the world needs, and what you can be rewarded for.

Finding your Ikigai requires introspection and reflection. It is not something that is discovered overnight, but an ongoing process of self-exploration and personal growth. Below I will guide you through a journey of discovering your Ikigai, helping you identify areas of your life that can lead to greater fulfillment and happiness.

1. Reflect on What You Love (Passion)

The first step to discovering your Ikigai is to reflect on what you love to do. Ask yourself:

- **What are you really passionate about?**Think about the activities that make you lose track of time, the ones that fill you with energy and satisfaction.
- **What are the hobbies or passions that make you happy?**These can be related to creativity, sports, music, writing, or any other activity that makes you feel alive.

2. Identify What You Are Good At (Talent)

The second step is to recognize what you are good at. Often, our passions align with our innate or developed abilities. Ask yourself:

- **What do you naturally excel at?**This could be something that others easily recognize about you, a talent or skill that sets you apart.
- **What are the skills that you have developed over time that give you satisfaction?**This could include professional, artistic, social or technical skills.

3. Exploring What the World Needs (Mission)

The third step is to think about what the world needs and how you can contribute. Ask yourself:

- **What are the needs of society that deeply touch you?**This could be about the environment, education, health, social justice, or any other cause you are passionate about.
- **How can you make a difference in the world with your skills and passions?**Think about how you can use your talents to address a real need, improving the lives of others.

4. Consider How You Can Be Rewarded (Profession/Vocation)

Finally, consider how you can be rewarded for what you do. This isn't just about money, but also about satisfaction and recognition. Ask yourself:

- **How can you make a living doing what you love?**Consider opportunities to turn your passion into a career or calling.
- **What are the professions or roles that allow you to express your talents and at the same time contribute to society?**Think about how you can find a balance between personal satisfaction and financial sustenance.

Practical Exercises to Discover Your Ikigai

Now that you have a clearer understanding of what constitutes Ikigai, here are some practical exercises that can help you identify yours and integrate it into your daily life.

Exercise 1: The Ikigai Diagram

Create a diagram of four intersecting circles, each representing one of the four elements of Ikigai: what you love, what you are good at, what the world needs, and what you can be rewarded for. Write your answers to each of the questions above in the circles and try to identify where these elements overlap. The point where all four circles meet represents your Ikigai.

Exercise 2: The Map of Passions

Make a list of all the activities you love to do, without censoring yourself. After you write down everything you are passionate about, try to connect these activities to your skills and the needs of the world. This will help you see how you can transform your passions into something bigger and more meaningful.

Exercise 3: The Ikigai Journal

Keep a journal to record the moments when you feel truly alive and fulfilled. What were you doing in those moments? What emotions did you feel? How can you do these activities more often in your daily life? Use this journal to reflect and to sharpen your understanding of your Ikigai.

Exercise 4: Conscious Actions

Every day, try to do at least one action that reflects your Ikigai. This could be something as simple as dedicating time to a passion, doing a kind thing for someone else, or working on a project that excites you. The important thing is to make these actions an integral part of your life.

Life Stories: Inspiring Ikigai Examples

To better understand how Ikigai can transform a person's life, let's look at some examples of individuals who have found and followed their Ikigai, bringing balance and happiness into their lives.

Story 1: The Okinawan Fisherman

In Okinawa, one of the so-called "blue zones" of the world, where the population is known for longevity and well-being, lives a man who has found his Ikigai in fishing. Every morning, he wakes up at dawn and goes to the sea. He does not fish to earn money, but for the pure pleasure of being in contact with nature and providing fresh food to his community. His passion for the sea, his skill in fishing, the need of his community and the recognition he receives combine perfectly, creating a deep sense of purpose that keeps him active and happy.

Story 2: The Calligraphy Master

A woman who has dedicated her life to the art of Japanese calligraphy has found her Ikigai in passing this ancient tradition on to new generations. Although it started as a hobby, calligraphy has become a way for her to express her creativity, connect with her cultural heritage, and teach others the importance of patience and beauty in detail. Today, her school is a place where people of all ages come to learn and find peace through writing, making a positive impact in their lives and communities.

Story 3: The Social Entrepreneur

A young entrepreneur, after a personal experience with poverty, decided to dedicate his life to solving the problem of lack of access to clean water in some of the most remote regions of the world. His passion for innovation, his technical skills, and the deep global need for safe water resources found a meeting point in his Ikigai. Today, he leads a foundation that develops sustainable technologies for access to water, improving the lives of thousands of people while finding deep personal satisfaction.

Finding your Ikigai is not just about discovery, but about living intentionally each day, cultivating the activities and relationships that give meaning and purpose to our existence. Through reflection, practical exercises, and inspiration from life stories, I hope you can get closer and closer to your Ikigai, finding the right balance between what you love, what you are good at, what the world needs, and what you can be rewarded for.

In the next chapter, we will explore the art of simplicity, discovering how eliminating the superfluous and living with essentiality can bring mental clarity and inner peace. Continue this journey of self-discovery, taking with you the sense of purpose that your Ikigai offers you.

Chapter 5: The Art of Simplicity (Kanso)

Essentiality: The importance of simplifying life by eliminating the superfluous

In the frenzy of modern life, we often find ourselves overwhelmed by excess: too many objects, too many commitments, too many distractions. This overload not only strains our physical space, but also our mind, creating a state of confusion and stress. This is where the Japanese concept of**Kanso**, which can be translated as "simplicity" or "essentiality".

Kanso invites us to reduce all that is superfluous, focusing on what is truly important. This principle is not only about physical minimalism, but also a mental approach to life, where value is found in simplicity and clarity. Removing the unnecessary allows us to free up space, not only externally, but also internally, bringing mental clarity, calm, and a greater ability to appreciate daily life.

How to apply Kanso in daily life:

6. **Review your priorities:** Take some time to reflect on what is truly important in your life. Are there activities, relationships, or objects that do not add value or joy? Consider reducing or eliminating them, focusing only on what brings you real satisfaction.
7. **Minimalism in objects:** Examine your physical spaces and reduce clutter. Donate or recycle what you no longer use or enjoy. Keep only what is functional and meaningful.
8. **Simplify your routines:** Look for ways to simplify your daily habits. For example, you could adopt a simpler morning routine or limit the number of activities in a day, focusing only on essential ones.

9. **Essentiality in relationships:** Evaluate your relationships and dedicate time and energy to the ones that really matter. Simplifying your social life doesn't mean isolating yourself, but cultivating authentic and meaningful relationships.

By applying the principle of Kanso, we can live with greater intentionality, appreciating what we have and reducing the stress caused by excess. This simplicity not only brings mental clarity, but also promotes a deep sense of inner peace.

Japanese Design and Aesthetics: Minimalism and the Use of Empty Spaces (Ma)

Japanese design is a reflection of the principle of Kanso and fully embraces minimalism and the intentional use of empty spaces, known as**But**. But it is not just the absence of objects, but a space that allows what exists to breathe and have greater meaning. This concept is applied in all forms of Japanese art, from architecture to painting, from the tea ceremony to haiku poetry.

Minimalism in Japanese Design:

Japanese minimalism is distinguished by its understated elegance, where each element is reduced to its purest essence. In traditional Japanese homes, interiors are often bare, with little furniture and decoration, but each element present is carefully chosen for its functionality and intrinsic beauty. This approach invites a quieter life, where space is not overfilled, but is left open to reflect and appreciate the value of simple things.

The concept of Ma:

Ma is the space that exists between things, both physically and conceptually. In a home, Ma might be the empty space between pieces of furniture, which allows the room to feel airy and not cluttered. In art, Ma is the silence between the notes of a melody or the white space on a page, which gives breath and meaning to words or images.

Applying Ma in everyday life means giving importance not only to what we do, but also to what we don't do. It is the art of knowing how to take breaks, of leaving empty spaces in our agendas, and of not filling every moment with frenetic activities. This space allows us to reflect, to rest and to find a deeper connection with ourselves and with what surrounds us.

How to Bring Minimalism and Ma into Life:

10. **Decluttering spaces:**Reduce the number of objects in your rooms. Keep only what is necessary and beautiful, and leave empty space to allow these objects to stand out. Empty space is not an absence, but a presence that invites reflection.
11. **Choose carefully:**Whenever you introduce a new element into your life, whether it is an object, an activity, or a relationship, ask yourself if it adds value and if it is in line with your principles of simplicity and essentiality.
12. **Break spaces:**Schedule breaks in your day. Allow for moments of silence and inactivity, allowing your mind to rest and regenerate.

13. **Appreciation of empty space:**Learn to see the value in what is not there. In a world that often celebrates the full and the frenetic, find beauty and meaning in the emptiness and the calm.

Mental Decluttering: Techniques to Bring Order to Your Mind and Emotions

The principle of Kanso and the concept of Ma apply not only to physical spaces, but also to our minds and emotions.**Mental Decluttering**means putting our thoughts in order, eliminating unnecessary worries, distractions and negative thoughts that weigh us down. Just like putting our house in order, putting our mind in order can also lead to greater clarity, focus and tranquility.

Mental Decluttering Techniques:

14. **Mindfulness practice:**Mindfulness, or awareness, is an essential practice for decluttering your mind. Set aside time each day to focus on the present, observing your thoughts without judgment. This will help you identify unhelpful or harmful thoughts and let them go.
15. **Writing a diary:**Keep a journal where you write down your thoughts and emotions. Writing allows you to express what is troubling you, to name your feelings, and to reflect on what is truly important. Once your thoughts are written down, you can review them more objectively and decide which ones are worthy of your attention.
16. **Make a to-do list:**Organizing your daily tasks into a list helps free your mind from having to remember everything. Simplify your lists by keeping them short and focused on what is a priority, and don't hesitate to delegate or postpone what is not urgent.
17. **Limit distractions:**Identify the main sources of distraction in your life, such as social media, phone notifications, or activities that don't really bring you satisfaction. Reduce the time you spend on these distractions, replacing them with more meaningful activities that align with your goals.

18. **Practice of "let go":** Learn the art of "let go," or letting go. There are thoughts and emotions that hold us back and weigh us down, often related to things we cannot change. Recognize what you cannot control and practice acceptance. This will free you from unnecessary weight, allowing you to focus on what you can actually influence.
19. **Meditation and conscious breathing:** Include meditation and mindful breathing in your daily routine. These practices help calm the mind, reduce anxiety, and bring greater clarity to your thoughts. Even a few minutes a day can make a big difference.

The Benefits of Mental Decluttering:

- **Better concentration:** An uncluttered mind is better able to focus on important tasks, improving productivity and effectiveness.
- **Stress Reduction:** Letting go of unnecessary thoughts reduces mental stress, creating a feeling of lightness and tranquility.
- **Greater clarity:** Decluttering your mind allows you to see things more clearly, making decision-making and problem-solving easier.

- **Personal Growth:** A mind free from distractions and unnecessary worries is more open to personal growth, creativity, and connection with oneself and others.

Conclusion of the Chapter

The art of simplicity, embodied by the principle of Kanso, teaches us that less is often more. Simplifying our lives, both in our physical spaces and in our minds, not only brings us clarity and inner peace, but also allows us to live with greater intentionality and appreciation for what truly matters.

In the next chapter, we will explore the way of tea and the awareness that this ancient Japanese practice can teach us, further integrating the principles of simplicity and presence into our daily lives.

Chapter 6: The Way of Tea - Ceremony and Awareness

Origins and Meaning

The Japanese tea ceremony, known as**Chanoyu**or**Chado**((the Way of Tea), is much more than a simple preparation and consumption of tea; it is a deeply rooted in Zen philosophy and Japanese culture, reflecting the values of simplicity, harmony and awareness.

The origins of the tea ceremony date back to the 9th century, when tea was introduced to Japan by Chinese Buddhist monks, who used it to stay awake during long meditation sessions. However, it was not until the Muromachi period (1336-1573) that the tea ceremony began to develop into the form we know today, thanks to the guidance of tea masters such as Murata Jukō and Sen no Rikyū. These masters infused the ceremony with deep spiritual meaning, transforming it into a path of self-cultivation and realization.

The tea ceremony is a perfect example of how a simple practice can be elevated to an art form and a moving meditation. Every gesture, every utensil and every word in the tea ceremony is imbued with meaning and follows precise rules that reflect the principles of harmony (wa), respect (kei), purity (sei) and tranquility (jaku). These principles not only guide the preparation and sharing of tea, but also the approach to daily life.

Taking part in a tea ceremony is an experience that invites you to detach yourself from the chaos of the outside world and enter a space of silence and reflection, where beauty is found in the details and in the present. It is not just the tea that is appreciated, but the entire experience of sharing, which promotes human connection and inner peace.

Life Lessons from the Tea Ceremony

The tea ceremony, with its attention to detail and deliberate pace, offers valuable lessons that can be applied to many aspects of life. Let's look at some of the main lessons we can learn from the Way of Tea.

1. Simplicity

The tea ceremony is a celebration of simplicity. The utensils used are basic and free of excessive ornamentation, and the tea room is often bare, with only a few carefully selected elements. This simplicity is not only aesthetic, but also a way to focus attention on what is truly important: the present moment, the tea, and the company.

Application to daily life: Simplicity in the tea ceremony teaches us to simplify our lives, eliminating the superfluous and focusing on what has value. We can apply this principle by simplifying our living space, our routines and our relationships, to live a lighter and more meaningful life.

2. Patience

Each stage of the tea ceremony requires patience and attention. Tea making is a slow and deliberate process, where every gesture is performed with care and respect. There is no rush, just calm, focused attention to the task at hand.

Application to daily life: In our fast-paced society, patience is often overlooked. The tea ceremony reminds us of the importance of slowing down, being patient, and allowing things to unfold at their natural pace. This patience can be applied in daily interactions, work, and relationships, cultivating greater peace and understanding.

3. Attention to Detail

Every aspect of the tea ceremony is carefully considered, from the movements of the tea master to the arrangement of the utensils. This attention to detail is not only an act of perfection, but an expression of respect and care for the overall experience.

Application to daily life: Bringing attention to detail into our daily lives means doing everything with awareness and intention, whether it's preparing a meal, writing a letter, or decorating your home. This care transforms ordinary activities into acts of beauty and meaning.

4. Harmony and Connection

The tea ceremony promotes a deep sense of harmony and connection, not only between participants, but also with the surrounding environment. The tea room, utensils, and outdoor garden are all integrated to create an experience of peace and unity.

Application to daily life: We can seek to create harmony in our lives by cultivating authentic relationships, respecting the environment, and living in harmony with our space. This may mean taking time to appreciate nature, building relationships based on mutual understanding and respect, and making life choices that reflect a balance between our needs and those of others.

Mindfulness Practices: Tea Ceremony Inspired Exercises

Incorporating the principles of the tea ceremony into our daily lives does not necessarily require becoming a tea master. Here are some practical exercises that can help you bring awareness and appreciation to the small moments of life, inspired by the Way of Tea.

1. The Daily Tea Ritual

Even if you don't follow a formal tea ceremony, you can create your own little daily ritual to prepare and enjoy a cup of tea with mindfulness. Take a few minutes a day to prepare the tea calmly, paying attention to each step: the water boiling, the steam rising, the aroma of the tea leaves. Sit in a quiet place and enjoy the tea without distractions, focusing only on the pleasure of the moment.

2. Taking Care of Your Space

Treat a space in your home as if it were a tea room. Keep this space simple and tidy, with a few objects that bring joy and tranquility. Every day, spend a few minutes cleaning and tidying this space, as an act of respect and awareness. This will help you cultivate a sense of calm and order that can positively influence the rest of your day.

3. Practice Silent Gratitude

During a tea ceremony, participants often silently express gratitude for the tea, the tea master, and the shared experience. Bring this practice into your daily life by taking moments of silence to express gratitude for the little things: the food you eat, the people you meet, the nature around you. This simple practice can transform your perspective and cultivate an attitude of ongoing appreciation.

4. Slow Down and Appreciate

Start slowing down your daily actions, doing one thing at a time with full attention. If you are cooking, focus only on that task, appreciating the color and texture of the ingredients. If you are walking, notice the rhythm of your steps and the contact of your feet with the ground. This conscious slowing down will help you live with greater presence and appreciation for the moment.

5. Create Moments of Silence

Just like in the tea ceremony, where silence is an integral part of the experience, create moments of silence in your day. You can start and end your day with a few minutes of silence, doing nothing, just sitting quietly and observing your thoughts and emotions. This restorative silence can help you center your mind and find greater inner peace.

Conclusion of the Chapter

The Way of Tea teaches us that true beauty and inner peace are found in simplicity, attention to detail, and mindful presence. By integrating the principles and practices inspired by the tea ceremony into our daily lives, we can cultivate a deeper sense of harmony, gratitude, and connection with ourselves and the world around us.

In the next chapter, we will explore Japonism and how Japanese aesthetics and values can offer us a unique lens to understand and interact with the world, further enriching our daily life experience.

Chapter 7: Understanding the World Through Japonism

Aesthetics and Nature: The importance of aesthetics in Japanese culture and the deep connection with nature

Japanese culture is renowned for its deep appreciation of aesthetics, a sensibility that is not only reflected in art and architecture, but permeates every aspect of daily life. This sense of aesthetics is closely linked to nature, with

with which the Japanese have developed a unique and harmonious relationship over the centuries.

One of the key concepts that embody this bond is**Shinrin Yoku**, which literally means "forest bathing." This practice, born in Japan in the 1980s, promotes spending time immersed in nature as a way to improve mental and physical health. But Shinrin-Yoku is much more than a simple walk in the woods; it is a way to reconnect with nature, to breathe in its essence, and to let yourself be enveloped by its calm and regenerating rhythm.

The practice of Shinrin-Yoku reflects a deeper truth in Japanese culture: nature is not seen as something to be dominated, but as an element to be lived in harmony with. This vision is also expressed in the art of Japanese gardening, where every stone, every plant and every element is placed with a precise intention to create a perfect balance with the surrounding environment.

Examples of aesthetics and nature in Japanese culture:

- **Zen Gardens:**Japanese Zen gardens are a perfect example of how aesthetics and nature can merge to create spaces for meditation and reflection. Every stone and every grain of sand has a meaning, representing mountains, rivers and seas, in a minimalist landscape that invites contemplation.

-

- **Hanami:**The tradition of Hanami, cherry blossom viewing, is another example of how the Japanese celebrate the fleeting beauty of nature. Every year, the cherry blossoms become a national event, a time to reflect on the transitory beauty of life and to share this moment with others.

-

This deep connection with nature and aesthetics is not just something to be admired from afar, but a principle we can adopt into our lives to find greater harmony and awareness.

The **Japonism** is a term that refers to the influence of Japanese art and culture on the West, particularly during the late 19th and early 20th centuries. However, Japonism can also be interpreted as a way of seeing and understanding the world through the lens of Japanese culture, embracing its aesthetic and philosophical values.

This approach can offer a unique perspective on how we interact with the world, emphasizing the importance of simplicity, natural beauty, and present-moment awareness. In a world often dominated by consumerism and frenzy, Japonism invites us to slow down, reflect, and find beauty in the everyday.

Key principles of Japonism to apply to life:

- **Wabi Sabi:** As discussed in previous chapters, Wabi-Sabi is the art of seeing beauty in imperfection and impermanence. Applying this principle to daily life means accepting and appreciating imperfections and changes, both in ourselves and in the world around us.
- **Mono not Aware:** This concept refers to the "sweet sadness of things," a deep appreciation of the ephemeral nature of life. Mono no Aware reminds us that everything, every moment is transitory, and therefore precious. This can help us live with greater awareness and gratitude, knowing that every experience is unique and unrepeatable.
- **But (blank space):** In Japanese design, the concept of Ma is the recognition of the importance of empty spaces, silence and pauses. In modern life, this can translate into creating spaces and moments of stillness, allowing ourselves to breathe, reflect and appreciate the natural rhythm of life.

By adopting these principles, we can develop a more balanced, harmonious way of living, in tune with the natural world and with ourselves.

Applying Japonism: Practical Advice

Here are some practical ways to incorporate Japanese aesthetic and philosophical principles into your daily life:

1. Create a Wabi-Sabi Space in Your Home

Dedicate a corner of your home to reflect the principles of Wabi-Sabi. Use natural materials such as wood, stone or ceramic, preferring objects that show the wear and tear of time. It could be a broken vase repaired with the art of kintsugi (gold repair), a potted plant that follows the cycle of the seasons, or an old chair that carries memories. This space will not only add beauty to your home, but will remind you every day to appreciate imperfection and impermanence.

2. Practice Shinrin-Yoku

Find a park, a forest or a garden where you can practice Shinrin-Yoku. Take some time to immerse yourself in nature, breathing deeply and observing the details around you. A long journey is not necessary; even just 20-30 minutes of immersion in nature can have beneficial effects on your mental and physical well-being.

3. Apply Mono no Aware to Your Everyday Experiences

Try to apply Mono no Aware in your daily interactions, remembering that each moment is unique and precious. Whether you are spending time with a loved one, watching a sunset or enjoying a meal, let the awareness of

The transience of these experiences increases your appreciation for them. This will help you live with greater presence and gratitude.

4. Integrate Ma into Your Days

Integrate the concept of Ma into your daily life by creating spaces of silence and pauses between activities. It can be as simple as a five-minute pause between meetings, or a half-hour of silence before bed. This quiet time will allow you to recharge your batteries and reflect, bringing a sense of balance and serenity to your day.

5. Reduce and Simplify

Embrace Japanese minimalism by reducing the unnecessary in your life. Simplify your environment, your routines, and even your thoughts, focusing on what is essential and meaningful. This will allow you to live with greater clarity and inner peace.

Conclusion of the Chapter

Japonism is not just an aesthetic appreciation for Japanese culture, but a lens through which we can see and interact with the world in a more profound and meaningful way. By adopting Japanese principles of aesthetics, simplicity, and connection to nature, we can enrich our daily lives, living with greater harmony, awareness, and gratitude.

In the next chapter, we will explore how to live with intent and serenity, integrating the concepts of Heijoshin, Kaizen, and Satori to constantly improve ourselves and find inner peace.

Shinrin-Yoku: Forest Bathing

Shinrin Yoku, which translates to "forest bathing," is a Japanese practice of immersing oneself in nature to promote mental and physical well-being. The practice requires no special effort or skill: it is simply a matter of spending time in a natural environment, breathing deeply, observing the beauty around you, and letting nature take its course.

The benefits of Shinrin-Yoku are supported by numerous scientific studies. Spending time in nature has been shown to be effective in reducing stress, lowering blood pressure, improving mood, and strengthening the immune system. Nature has a regenerative power on the mind and body, helping to restore balance and inner calm.

Scientific Benefits of Shinrin-Yoku:

20. **Stress Reduction:**Exposure to nature reduces levels of the stress hormone cortisol in the body. This contributes to a feeling of calm and relaxation.

21. **Mood Improvement:**Time spent outdoors increases levels of serotonin, the neurotransmitter linked to happiness and well-being, counteracting symptoms of depression and anxiety.

22. **Strengthening the Immune System:**Trees release essential oils called phytoncides, which have been shown to increase the activity of NK (natural killer) cells, improving the body's ability to fight off infection and disease.

23. **Improved Concentration:**Walking in nature helps restore concentration and attention, which is especially useful for those who do intense mental work.

Even in urban environments, it is possible to adapt the practice of Shinrin-Yoku. If you do not have access to a forest or a large park, look for smaller green spaces such as botanical gardens, city parks, or even green terraces. The important thing is to find a place where you can connect with nature, even if only for a few minutes a day.

Adapting Shinrin-Yoku into Urban Environments:

- **Visit Local Parks Regularly:**Even a short 20-30 minute walk in an urban park can offer many of the same benefits as traditional Shinrin-Yoku.

- **Creating a Nature Corner at Home:**If the weather doesn't allow you to go outside, bring nature inside. Grow plants, create a small garden, or even just open a window to let in natural light and fresh air.
- **Routine Integration:**Consider walking through green spaces on your way to work or running errands. Even brief interactions with nature throughout the day can make a big difference in your well-being.

Harnessing the Energy of the Universe

In Japanese philosophy, the concept of**You**(also called Qi or Chi) refers to the life energy that pervades the entire universe. It is believed that this energy can be cultivated and directed to promote physical, mental and spiritual well-being. Attuning to Ki means living in harmony with natural forces, maintaining a balanced flow of energy in and out of the body.

Techniques to Harness Ki:

24. Meditation to Tune in to Ki: or
> **Position and Breathing:**Sit in a comfortable position with your back straight. Close your eyes and begin to breathe deeply and slowly.

Imagine breathing in the life energy of the universe, filling your body with light and vitality with every inhalation.

or **Energy Flow Visualization:**Imagine the Ki flowing through your body, starting at the top of your head and moving down to your feet. Visualize this energy dissolving blockages or tension, leaving you feeling calm and renewed.

25. Breathing Exercises (Ki Breathing): or

Deep Breathing: Inhale slowly through your nose, filling your diaphragm and visualizing the energy entering your body. Hold for a few seconds, then exhale slowly through your mouth, releasing all tension.

or **Hara Breathing:**Focus your attention on the**Hara**((the lower abdominal area, considered the energy center of the body). Inhale deeply, imagining that the energy is accumulating in this area, and then exhale, spreading the energy throughout the body.

26. Tai Chi or Qi Gong: or

These Chinese practices are closely related to the concept of Ki and consist of slow, flowing movements combined with deep, conscious breathing. Tai Chi and Qi Gong are excellent for balancing Ki, improving flexibility, strength, and mental health. If you don't have access to a

or teacher or a class, there are many online videos that can introduce you to these practices, allowing you to start working with Ki in the comfort of your own home.

Tuning Into the Energy of Nature:

Ki flows not only within our bodies, but also around us in nature. Spending time outside, walking barefoot on the grass, or simply sitting near a tree can help you tune into natural energy and recharge your Ki.

Conclusion:

Understanding and making use of the world around us is not just about interacting with nature, but also about integrating Japanese aesthetic principles into our lives and tuning into universal energies. By following these practices, you can live with greater harmony, awareness and well-being, reconnecting not only with yourself, but also with the universe around you.

Chapter 9: Living with Intent and Serenity

Heijoshin - The Unperturbed Mind

Heijōshin is a Japanese concept that translates as "unperturbed mind" or "calm mind." It is the ability to maintain a stable and serene mind, regardless of external circumstances. This state of mind is especially revered in Japanese martial arts, where inner calm is essential for making quick and accurate decisions, even under pressure.

In the context of daily life, Heijoshin represents the ability to remain centered and calm in the face of adversity, without being overwhelmed by emotions or events. Cultivating an unperturbed mind does not mean suppressing emotions, but developing the ability to observe situations with detachment, reacting thoughtfully rather than impulsively.

Techniques for cultivating Heijoshin:

27. **Regular Meditation:** Meditation practice, especially Zazen meditation, is one of the most effective tools for developing Heijoshin. Sitting quietly, observing your thoughts, and letting them go without attachment helps cultivate a calm and stable mind.
28. **Conscious breathing:** When you find yourself in a stressful or tense situation, focus on your breathing. Take slow, deep breaths, focusing on the rhythm of your breathing. This simple act can calm your nervous system and bring your mind back to a state of balance.
29. **Daily Calm Rituals:** Integrate small rituals into your day that promote serenity, such as drinking a cup of tea in silence, taking a walk in nature, or taking a few minutes to read an inspiring book. These moments of quiet help maintain an unruffled mind.

30. **Positive view:** When you feel that negative emotions are taking over, practice positive visualization. Imagine a place or situation that gives you calm and serenity, and focus on this image until you feel your mind relax.

31. **Acceptance:** A fundamental part of Heijoshin is to accept situations as they are, without trying to change or control them. Learn to accept what you cannot change, focusing on how you can respond in a positive and constructive way.

By applying these techniques, you can develop a mind capable of maintaining balance even in the most difficult circumstances, living with greater serenity and emotional control.

Kaizen is a Japanese term meaning "change for the better" or "continuous improvement." This concept has been widely adopted in business, especially in manufacturing, as a systematic approach to improving processes and products. However, Kaizen can also be applied on a personal level, becoming a philosophy of life that promotes constant and progressive improvement.

The core principle of Kaizen is that improvement does not come through big changes, but rather through small, consistent adjustments that, over time, lead to significant progress. This mindset applies to all aspects of life: from career to personal development, from relationships to health.

How to apply Kaizen in daily life:

32. **Small, achievable goals:** Start by setting small daily goals that are easily achievable. For example, if you want to improve your fitness, start with five minutes of exercise a day and gradually increase the time. These small steps will help you build sustainable habits in the long run.

33. **Daily Reflection:** Every day, take a few minutes to reflect on what you have done well and what you could improve. This reflection allows you to identify areas where you can make small changes to constantly improve.

34. **Adopting a growth mindset:** Embrace the growth mindset, recognizing that every experience, positive or negative, is an opportunity to learn and grow. This attitude will help you see small steps forward as successes, rather than focusing only on the big milestones.

35. **Improvement routine:** Create a routine that encourages continuous improvement. This can include reading daily, learning a new skill, or working on personal projects. The important thing is to do something every day that brings you closer to your goals.
36. **Constant feedback:** Seek feedback regularly, both from yourself and others. Listening to constructive criticism and making adjustments based on feedback is essential for continuous improvement.

Applying the Kaizen principle helps you live with intentionality, focusing on constant and progressive improvement that, over time, will lead to significant changes in your personal and professional life.

Satori - The Sudden Enlightenment

Satori is a key concept in Zen Buddhism and refers to a sudden moment of enlightenment or realization. While Zen practice often emphasizes gradual work and discipline (as seen in Kaizen), Satori represents those moments when a deep and immediate understanding of truth is achieved in a flash.

This state of sudden awareness is often described as a feeling of absolute clarity, where illusions fall away and one perceives reality for what it really is. Although Satori is traditionally associated with spiritual experiences, it can occur at any time in life, often unexpectedly, during a daily activity or deep reflection.

How to Recognize and Foster Satori Moments:

37. **Practice presence:** Satori often occurs when we are fully present and aware of the present moment. Cultivating mindfulness in your

everyday activities can pave the way for these experiences of sudden enlightenment.

38.**Welcome the unexpected:**Be open to life's surprises. Sometimes Satori happens at the most unexpected times, when we let go and allow life to happen without trying to control it.

39.**Deep Meditation:**Meditation, especially the practice of Zazen, can create the conditions for the experience of Satori. During meditation, the mind can become so calm and clear that a simple thought or observation can bring about an explosion of awareness.

40.**Reflection on the meaning:**Spend time reflecting on life's big questions: Who am I? What is my purpose? What is the true nature of reality? These moments of introspection can lead to profound and sudden realizations.

41.**Acceptance of not knowing:**Satori often comes when we let go of the need to understand everything rationally and accept the mystery of life. Let the questions remain open and allow understanding to emerge naturally.

Examples of Satori in daily life:

- **A moment of understanding:**Imagine being in a stressful situation and suddenly realizing that your stress comes not from the situation itself but from your attachment to a particular outcome. In an instant, you feel liberated, and the situation seems to transform before your eyes.
- **A moment of deep connection:**You may be in the company of someone and, for no apparent reason, suddenly feel connected to that person and to the world in a whole new way. It's as if the barrier between you and others disappears, revealing a sense of oneness.
- **Beauty in simplicity:**You may be engaged in a mundane activity, like washing dishes, and suddenly realize the intrinsic beauty of that moment, the connection between you, the water, and the entire universe. This is Satori: a moment of enlightenment that transforms your perception of reality.

Living with intent and serenity means cultivating an unperturbed mind through Heijoshin, constantly improving ourselves with Kaizen, and being open to moments of sudden enlightenment with Satori. Together, these Japanese concepts offer us guidance for living a more mindful, balanced, and meaningful life.

In the next and final chapter, we reflect on everything we've explored throughout the book, offering practical advice for maintaining balance and continuous improvement in your daily life, and providing additional resources for further exploring these teachings.

Conclusion: A New Beginning

Final Reflection

Dear reader,

We took a journey together through Japanese philosophy, exploring the principles that guide a life of balance, serenity and awareness. From the concept of **How**, harmony in all things, until the discovery of one's own**Ikigai**, passing through the practice of simplicity with**Kanso**and attention to detail in the**Tea Street**, each chapter offered tools and reflections to enrich your daily life.

Now, having come to the end of this journey, it is time to look forward and think about how you can carry these teachings with you on your personal journey. Japanese philosophy, with its profound wisdom and practical applicability, is not just a set of concepts to be learned, but a way of life that can transform your approach to life.

Continue Your Personal Growth Journey

Personal growth is not an end point, but an ongoing process, a lifelong journey. Every day offers new opportunities to apply what you've learned, to explore new aspects of your mind and heart, and to improve yourself in small but meaningful ways.

Here are some ways you can continue to cultivate your personal growth by integrating the teachings of Japanese philosophy:

42. **Live with Intention:**Remember that every action, every decision, can be made with intention and awareness. Be present in each moment and choose to act in a way that reflects your values   and purpose.
43. **Cultivate Inner Serenity:**Practice meditation or other forms of mindfulness regularly to maintain a calm and unruffled mind. Heijoshin, the unruffled mind, will help you navigate the storms of life with greater serenity.

44. **Embrace Continuous Improvement:**Apply the Kaizen philosophy in your daily life. Remember that every day is an opportunity to make small improvements, which over time will accumulate into significant changes.
45. **Be Open to Moments of Enlightenment:**Keep an open and receptive mind, ready to catch those moments of Satori, those sudden realizations that can change your perspective on life. These moments often come when you least expect them, but they can have a lasting impact.
46. **Appreciate the Beauty of Imperfection:**Integrate the principle of Wabi-Sabi into your life, finding beauty in imperfection and impermanence. This will allow you to accept yourself and others with greater compassion and see the value in every experience, even the difficult ones.
47. **Connect with Nature:**Reconnect with nature through practices such as Shinrin-Yoku and Hanami. Nature will not only offer you peace and regeneration, but will also remind you of your place in a larger world, where everything is interconnected.

A New Beginning

Even though this book is coming to an end, the real journey begins now, with you. The lessons you have learned are tools you can take with you on your journey, tools that will help you live a more balanced, conscious, and meaningful life.

Every day is a new opportunity to begin, to apply what you have learned, and to continue to grow. No matter how small a step it may seem, each step brings you closer to your Ikigai, your deepest purpose. Remember that the journey is as important as the destination.

As you continue on your journey, I hope you take with you a sense of serenity and purpose, knowing that Japanese philosophy offers you reliable guidance for meeting life's challenges with grace and wisdom.

Thank you for sharing this journey with me. May you find harmony, peace and fulfillment every step of the way.

Additional Resources

If you want to further deepen your understanding of Japanese philosophy and continue to grow, here are some resources I recommend:

- **Books:**Continue exploring Japanese wisdom with recommended readings such as "The Book of Tea" by Okakura Kakuzō, "Zen and the Art of Motorcycle Maintenance" by Robert M. Pirsig, and "Kaizen: The Key to Japan's Competitive Success" by Masaaki Imai.
- **Documentaries and Films:**Watch documentaries about Japanese culture, such as "Jiro Dreams of Sushi," which explores the life philosophy of a sushi master, or "Baraka," a film that captures the beauty of nature and human life.
- **Courses and Workshops:**Attend workshops or courses in Zen meditation, tea ceremony, or mindfulness practices. These experiences can give you a deeper and more practical understanding of the teachings explored in this book.

I wish you the best in your continued journey of growth and discovery.

Conclusion

Completing this book is just the beginning of a new chapter in your life. Take the teachings of Japanese philosophy with you, apply them with intention and serenity, and you will discover a new way of living that will bring you greater balance, happiness, and fulfillment.

Call to Action: Maintaining Balance and Continuous Improvement in Everyday Life

Now that you have explored the fundamental concepts of Japanese philosophy and gained new perspectives on how to live a more balanced and meaningful life, it is time to put what you have learned into practice. The true value of these teachings comes when we integrate them into our daily lives, making awareness, intentionality, and continuous improvement part of our way of being.

Here are some practical tips to maintain balance and promote continuous improvement every day:

1. Start Your Day with Intention

Every morning, take a few minutes to define your intentions for the day. Ask yourself:

- What are the three main things I want to accomplish today?
- How can I face challenges with serenity and an unperturbed mind?
- What can I do to improve myself, even just one small step?

This simple ritual will help you start with clarity and determination, keeping your focus on what is truly important.

2. Practice Daily Mindfulness

Integrate mindfulness into your daily activities. Whether you're washing dishes, walking, or working, bring your attention to the present moment. Notice details, notice sensations, and allow yourself to be fully present in each action. This not only reduces stress, but helps you live with greater awareness and appreciation.

3. Implement Personal Kaizen

Adopt the Kaizen philosophy of continuous improvement in your personal life. Identify an area you want to improve, be it your health, your career, or your relationships. Take small steps each day to progress in that direction. For example, if you want to improve your physical fitness, start with 10 minutes of exercise a day and gradually increase the time.

4. Create Spaces of Simplicity and Serenity

Designate an area of your home or office as a space of simplicity, where you can retreat to find calm and focus. Keep this space free of clutter and fill it only with objects that bring you joy and peace. Use this space for meditation, reading, or simply quiet reflection.

5. Cultivate Relationships with Intentionality

Apply the principles of Japonism to your relationships. Be present and listen attentively when interacting with others. Show respect and gratitude, and seek to build authentic and meaningful connections. Relationships based on these principles tend to be stronger and more lasting.

6. Reconnect with Nature

Take time regularly to immerse yourself in nature, following the concept of Shinrin-Yoku. Even a short walk in a park or sitting under a tree can rejuvenate your mind and spirit, helping you find balance and connection with the natural world.

7. Reflect and Recalibrate

At the end of each day or week, take time to reflect on your progress and learnings. Ask yourself what you did well and what you could do differently. This regular reflection will help you stay on track with your goals and make adjustments as needed to maintain continuous improvement.

Suggestions for Further Reading and Practice

To continue exploring and integrating Japanese philosophy into your life, here are some resources I recommend:

Books:

- **""The Book of Tea" by Okakura Kakuzō:** A classic that explores Japanese philosophy and culture through the tea ceremony, offering a profound understanding of simplicity and beauty.
- **"Kaizen: The Key to Japan's Competitive Success" by Masaaki Imai:** A comprehensive introduction to the concept of Kaizen and its application, not only in business, but also in everyday life.
- **"Wabi-Sabi: For Artists, Designers, Poets & Philosophers" by Leonard Koren:** This book explores the concept of Wabi-Sabi and how it can influence art, design and our outlook on life.

Documentaries and Films:

- **"Jiro Dreams of Sushi":** A documentary that follows the life of Jiro Ono, an 85-year-old sushi master, exploring his dedication to the art of sushi and his commitment to continuous improvement.
- **"Baraka":** A visually stunning documentary film that explores the relationship between humanity and nature, offering a visual meditation on the beauty and fragility of the world.

Practices and Workshops:

- **Zen Meditation:** Find a Zen meditation center in your area or take an online course to deepen your practice of Zazen meditation and mindfulness.

- **Tea Ceremony Workshop:** Attending a tea ceremony workshop can offer a firsthand experience of this ancient ritual and a deeper understanding of Japanese culture.
- **Art of Kintsugi:** Consider learning the art of Kintsugi, the Japanese practice of repairing broken pottery with gold, symbolizing the beauty of imperfection and healing.

Conclusion

Maintaining balance and continuous improvement requires intentionality, commitment, and the willingness to apply what you have learned in your daily life. With practical advice and the suggested resources, you can continue to grow and develop, living a life full of meaning, serenity and fulfillment.

Remember, the journey to balance and personal growth is an ongoing process, but every small step you take brings you closer to living in harmony with yourself and the world around you.

May this be a new beginning for you, full of discoveries and serenity.

Appendices

Glossary of Japanese Terms

Bushido ((English translation):

The "Warrior Code" of the samurai, a philosophy of life that emphasizes values   such as righteousness, courage, benevolence, respect, sincerity, honor and loyalty. Bushidō guides not only in martial arts, but also in behavior and personal discipline.

Chanoyu ((English translation):

Also known as "The Way of Tea," it is the Japanese tea ceremony, a ritual of preparing and drinking tea that emphasizes harmony, respect, purity, and tranquility. It is a practice that reflects Zen values   and simplicity.

Heijōshin ((English:

A term that translates as "unperturbed mind" or "calm mind." It refers to the ability to maintain a stable and calm mind even when faced with difficult or stressful situations.

Ikigai ((English translation):

Concept that represents the "reason for being" or the "reason why you get up in the morning." It is the intersection of what you love, what you are good at, what the world needs, and what you can be rewarded for.

Kaizen ((in Italian):

A term meaning "continuous improvement." In personal and professional settings, Kaizen refers to the practice of making small, consistent improvements that, over time, lead to significant progress.

Kanso ((in Italian):

One of the seven Japanese aesthetic principles, meaning "simplicity" or "essentiality." Kanso emphasizes the elimination of the superfluous to reveal the beauty and purity of things.

Kintsugi ((in Italian):

Japanese art of repairing broken ceramic objects with gold, enhancing the cracks and breaks as part of the object's history, rather than hiding them. Symbolizes the beauty of imperfection and healing.

But (間):

A concept that refers to empty space or the gap between things. In design, Ma is the deliberate use of space to create balance and harmony. In life, it represents the importance of silence and pauses.

Mono not Aware ((English translation):

An expression that indicates the "sweet sadness of things" or the awareness of the transience of life. It is a feeling of empathy and appreciation for the ephemeral and temporary beauty of the world.

Satori ((in Italian):

A Zen Buddhist term referring to sudden enlightenment or profound realization. It is a moment of clarity in which one understands the true nature of reality.

Shinrin Yoku ((English translation):

Literally "forest bathing," it is a Japanese practice of spending time immersed in nature to promote mental and physical well-being. It is a form of outdoor meditation that encourages reconnection with nature.

Wabi Sabi ((English):

A Japanese aesthetic concept that finds beauty in imperfection, impermanence, and incompleteness. Wabi-Sabi celebrates simplicity and authenticity, accepting the transitory nature of life.

Zanshin ((in Italian):

A term that translates as "remaining mind" or "persistent awareness." In martial arts and daily life, Zanshin refers to a state of continued alertness and presence, even after an action has been completed.

Zazen ((in Italian):

A form of seated meditation practiced in Zen Buddhism. Zazen is the central practice of Zen, in which one seeks to achieve awareness and enlightenment through silent meditation and focus on the breath.

Additional Resources

Books:

- **""The Book of Tea" by Okakura Kakuzō:**A classic that explores the cultural and philosophical importance of the tea ceremony, offering a deep insight into Japanese culture and simplicity.
- **"Wabi-Sabi: For Artists, Designers, Poets & Philosophers" by Leonard Koren:** An in-depth exploration of the concept of Wabi-Sabi and how this aesthetic influences art, design and everyday life.
- **"Kaizen: The Key to Japan's Competitive Success" by Masaaki Imai:**A comprehensive guide to the concept of Kaizen, with practical applications in both business and personal growth.
- **"The Art of Simple Living: 100 Daily Practices from a Japanese Zen Monk for a Lifetime of Calm and Joy" by Shunmyo Masuno:**A book that offers daily practices inspired by Zen philosophy to live a calmer and more joyful life.
- **"Zen Mind, Beginner's Mind" by Shunryu Suzuki:**A fundamental introductory text on Zen Buddhism, exploring the practice of meditation and the beginner's mind as a path to enlightenment.

Documentaries and Films:

- **"Jiro Dreams of Sushi":**A documentary that follows the life of Jiro Ono, an 85-year-old sushi master, exploring his dedication to the art of sushi and the concept of continuous improvement.

- **"Baraka":**A documentary film that explores the relationship between humanity and nature, capturing the beauty and fragility of the world in extraordinary images.
- **"The Birth of Sake":**A documentary that explores the ancient Japanese tradition of sake brewing, offering a reflection on respect for tradition and art.

Websites and Articles:

- **Tofu (www.tofugu.com):**A website that offers insights into Japanese culture, language, and traditions. A great resource for those who want to further explore Japonism and other aspects of Japanese life.
- **Zen Habits (www.zenhabits.net):**A blog dedicated to simplicity and mindfulness, with numerous articles on how to apply Zen principles to daily life.
- **The Art of Kintsugi:**Articles and online resources on how to learn the art of Kintsugi and apply it as a metaphor in healing and finding beauty in imperfections.

Workshops and Courses:

- **Zen Meditation Courses:**Find Zen meditation centers in your area or explore online courses that offer introductions to Zazen practice and Zen philosophy.
- **Tea Ceremony Workshop:**Attending a tea ceremony workshop can give you a first-hand experience of the Way of Tea and a deeper understanding of Japanese culture.
- **Japanese Calligraphy Lessons:**Learning Japanese calligraphy can be a way to immerse yourself in Japanese aesthetic culture and practice calmness and precision.

Diaries and Practical Exercises

This section is designed to help you reflect on and apply the concepts you learn in the book to your daily life. Use it as a personal space where you can write down your thoughts, do practical exercises, and monitor your progress. Take your time to complete these exercises calmly, and return to these pages whenever you feel the need to reflect or recalibrate your path.

1. Your Ikigai Journal

Discover Your Ikigai:

48. What You Love:

or   Make a list of activities that you are passionate about, that make you feel alive and that give you energy. Write down everything that comes to mind, without censoring yourself.

or Which of these activities could you do every day without getting
or tired? What makes you lose track of time?

49. What are you good at:

or   List the skills and talents you have developed throughout your life. These can be related to work, hobbies, or other experiences. In what areas do
or you receive compliments from others?
or What are your unique skills that set you apart?

50. What the World Needs: or

Identify issues or needs in society that deeply affect
you. What causes are close to your heart?

or How can you contribute to solving these problems with your skills and passions?

51. What You Can Be Rewarded For: or

List ways you could get paid or recognized for what you love to do and are good at.

or What careers, jobs, or vocations align with your passions and skills?

Summary of Your Ikigai:

- In light of the above answers, try to describe your Ikigai in a sentence or a short paragraph.

For example: "My Ikigai is to help people improve their mental health through creative writing, combining my passion for writing and my interest in psychological well-being."

- Write your Ikigai here:

2. Simplicity Exercises and Mental Decluttering

Physical Decluttering:

52. Personal Space:
or Choose a room or corner of your home that you want to simplify. Which items are essential and which can be eliminated?

or What can you donate, recycle, or throw away to create a more orderly and peaceful environment?

53. Your Space of Serenity: or
Create a small space in your home dedicated to peace and reflection. What elements bring you calm and joy?

or Describe how this space looks and feels.

Mental Decluttering:

54. Identify Your Distractions: or
What are the main sources of distraction in your daily life? (e.g., social media, television, multitasking)

or How can you limit or eliminate these distractions to improve your focus and peace of mind?

55. Mindfulness Practice: or
Spend a few minutes each day practicing mindfulness. What daily activity can you turn into a moment of mindfulness? (e.g., washing dishes, walking, drinking a cup of tea)

or Describe your experience with mindfulness. How does it feel to be fully present in an activity?

3. Awareness Journal (Zanshin)

Reflection on Presence:

56. Zanshin Moments: or
Describe a recent situation in which you felt completely present and aware. How did you feel physically, emotionally, and mentally at that moment?

or What have you noticed that is different than when you act automatically or distractedly?

57. Application of Zanshin: or
What daily activities can benefit from increased presence and awareness? Choose a specific activity to practice Zanshin each day this week.

or Describe the results and sensations that emerge from this practice.

4. Kaizen Diary: Continuous Improvement

Kaizen Goals:

58. Identify an Area for Improvement: or

What area of your personal or professional life would you like to improve? (e.g., fitness, time management, relationships) What are or small steps you can take each day to improve in this area?

59. Progress Monitoring: or

Every day, take note of the small steps you make. Even if they are small, every step counts.

or What have you learned from the continuous improvement process? What adjustments can you make?

5. Moments of Satori: Sudden Enlightenment

Reflection on Sudden Realizations:

60. Describe a Satori Moment: or

Remember a time when you had a sudden realization that changed your perspective on something. What circumstances led up to that moment?

or How has this realization influenced your way of thinking or living?

61. Foster New Moments of Satori: or

What practices or reflections can you cultivate to encourage the emergence of new moments of Satori? (e.g., meditation, reading, time in nature)

or Keep track of any new moments of enlightenment and how they are changing your life.

These journals and practice exercises are designed to help you integrate the concepts explored in the book into your daily life. Keep them as a companion along the way, returning to reflect on them periodically to track your progress and continue to grow.

Final Reflection

Together we journeyed through the rich philosophy of Japan, exploring the principles that can guide you toward a life of greater balance, awareness, and serenity. From the art of simplicity and continuous improvement, to a deep connection with nature and finding your Ikigai, each concept we explored is a piece that, once integrated into your life, can contribute to a lasting transformation.

But it is important to remember that the journey to self-understanding and inner balance has no final destination. It is an ongoing journey, a dance between growth and reflection, between action and pause, between acceptance and improvement. Transformation does not happen all at once, but through small daily steps, conscious choices, and moments of reflection that, over time, accumulate to lead to significant changes.

As you close this book, I invite you to take the lessons you have learned with you, integrating them into your life so that they become part of your being. Whether you are beginning to explore your Ikigai, practicing mindfulness in your daily activities, or seeking beauty in imperfection, remember that every step forward, no matter how small, is progress toward a more harmonious and meaningful life.

A New Beginning

This is not just the end of a book, but the beginning of a new chapter in your life. A chapter where you have the opportunity to live with greater awareness, intention, and gratitude. It is not about achieving perfection, but about living in harmony with yourself and the world around you, embracing each day as an opportunity to grow and improve.

I invite you to do your best every day, not only for yourself, but for those around you and for the entire world. Japanese philosophy teaches us that true beauty lies in imperfection, that serenity is an art to be cultivated, and that personal growth is a journey that never ends.

Start each day with intention, live each moment with awareness, and end each evening with gratitude. By doing so, you will transform not only your life, but also the world around you, step by step, with grace and wisdom.

Thank you for sharing this journey. May you continue to explore, grow, and find your balance, living with fullness and serenity.

Printed in Great Britain
by Amazon

54787244R00036